How Should I Think?

Crucial Questions booklets provide a quick introduction to definitive Christian truths. This expanding collection includes titles such as:

Who Is Jesus?

Can I Trust the Bible?

Does Prayer Change Things?

Can I Know God's Will?

How Should I Live in This World?

What Does It Mean to Be Born Again?

Can I Be Sure I'm Saved?

What Is Faith?

What Can I Do with My Guilt?

What Is the Trinity?

TO BROWSE THE REST OF THE SERIES,
PLEASE VISIT: LIGONIER.ORG/CQ

CQ

How Should I Think?

R.C. SPROUL

 LIGONIER MINISTRIES

How Should I Think?
© 2021 by the R.C. Sproul Trust

Published by Ligonier Ministries
421 Ligonier Court, Sanford, FL 32771
Ligonier.org

Printed in China
RR Donnelley
0000122
First printing

ISBN 978-1-64289-332-8 (Paperback)
ISBN 978-1-64289-333-5 (ePub)
ISBN 978-1-64289-334-2 (Kindle)

Cover design: Ligonier Creative
Interior typeset: Katherine Lloyd, The DESK

Library of Congress Control Number: 2021931286

Contents

Chapter One

What Is the Mind?

One day I was eating a meal, and I had some watermelon on my plate. I was thinking deeply about the significance of this watermelon because I happened to be on a diet program that seeks to balance proteins, fats, and carbohydrates. I was thinking, "This is a carbohydrate." I used to just think of it as a fruit, but now I understood it was a carbohydrate, and I had to determine whether it was a favorable carbohydrate or an unfavorable carbohydrate. I discovered it was a favorable carbohydrate, whose substance would be converted into fructose in the bloodstream. As I was doing all this analysis of the value of watermelon, I wondered what the piece of watermelon was thinking as it was about to be devoured. Of course, we laugh at that because we make the initial assumption that watermelons can't think. They're not animals; they're plants. And there are few, if any, people who would imagine that this piece of watermelon could contemplate its eater.

In the history of philosophy, however, not everyone has agreed with the assumption that watermelons can't think. For example, the rationalist philosopher Gottfried Leibniz developed an intricate system called monadology. He believed that all forms of matter had some capacity for what we call "thinking," even if this thinking would be reduced to what he called "petite perceptions." For the most part, his theory of petite perceptions did not make that much of an impact on the intellectual world. And as I said, few, if any, people since have considered the possibility of plants thinking.

So how do we really know whether plants can think? How do we know if animals can think? When I say something to my dog, his customary response is to cock his head to one side and look at me with a puzzled look on his face. Sometimes it seems that our pets and other animals have some kind of ability to think; however, the typical assessment of the scientific world is that these animals don't actually think. They simply respond to external stimuli by a force that is somewhat loosely called instinct.

So what is the difference between instinct and thought? That question has been probed by researchers, and people have come to various conclusions. On the one hand, some say that when we say that what animals do is "mere instinct" and not "thought," that reflects a certain arrogance of the human species; we assume that we are the only creature that has the ability or capacity for discursive thinking. On the other hand, some argue that animals do have the ability to think, though perhaps not at the same advanced level that human beings have.

Then there are those who say that what we call "thinking" as human beings is nothing more than instinct, that it is nothing more than a biochemical reaction to stimuli. This raises one of the oldest philosophical questions that thinkers have considered: What is the mind?

One theologian would play a word game in seeking to answer that question. He would ask, "What is the mind?"

And he would reply, "No matter." And then when somebody said, "Well, what is matter?" he said, "Never mind." He was trying to communicate that though we recognize that the mind is inseparably related to something material and physical such as the brain, what we call the "mind" cannot be absolutely equated with the brain. The brain may be the seat of the mind, and it may be the organ that the body uses to think, but there is a difference between the physical organ that does the thinking and the thinking itself.

And so we ask the questions: What is thought? Is thought merely a biochemical electrical impulse that can be measured in pure physical categories, or is there something spiritual and nonphysical about this thing that is so basic to our existence as human beings? We know we are people who think and who have ideas in what we call our minds. We have a tendency to locate the source of that thinking in our heads. We also know that physical injuries to the brain can alter patterns of thought, as can chemical imbalances in the brain.

We make distinctions with respect to what is called mental illness, where people lose the capacity to think in a rational manner. And yet, people who are deemed to be perfectly healthy mentally also at times think in an irrational manner, and so we often wonder where that line is between mental illness and mental soundness, between sanity and insanity. It's often been said that there's a thin line between genius and insanity, between those who think at extraordinary depths and those who somehow cross the border into madness. We've seen an unusually high rate of insanity among some of the most celebrated thinkers of world history. That thin line between genius and insanity is one that we sometimes see people skating back and forth over.

What is the mind? It's not a simple question to answer. When we are awake, is there ever a time when we're not thinking? We may not be thinking in a deep logical order or analysis. We may be daydreaming, but even while we're daydreaming, we're having thoughts. We're having ideas that we're aware of. We're in a state of consciousness. But then we also experience the phenomenon of thinking when we're asleep, when sometimes the train of thought or the stream of consciousness takes some wild and bizarre turns. We've all experienced what we call a nightmare, where the thinking in the midst of our sleep frightens us.

These experiences multiply the difficulty of sorting out

exactly what it means to have a mind and to think. Now, for our consideration as Christians, we have to understand that the bottom line is that the Scriptures assume that inherent in our humanity is the ability to think. And the claim of sacred Scripture is that we are moral beings.

To be a moral being, one has to have the ability to behave in a way that is in correspondence with or opposition to some moral standard. And the standard in Scripture is the law of God. The God of the Bible is a God who holds us accountable for our obedience or disobedience to His law. To be a creature who is responsible for one's behavior morally is to be a moral being.

What else is required to be a moral being? We've thought that through in the history of the church again and again. We conclude that a necessary condition for being a moral being is to have a will. That is, moral creatures must be volitional creatures. They must have the power, ability, and capacity to make choices, to make decisions. We are creatures who possess a will.

Then we ask the even more problematic question, What is the will? Jonathan Edwards, who I believe wrote the most important book dealing with this question of the nature and function of the human will, *The Freedom of the Will*, once defined the will in simple terms. He said, "The will is the mind choosing." In order for a person to exercise his or her will, to make a choice that is of a moral kind, that person has to be in some state of awareness. What you do when you are unconscious is not something that we normally consider to be of a moral nature. We understand that when it comes to our bodily functions, we distinguish between those that are voluntary and those that are involuntary. We don't choose every second to have our hearts beat and push blood throughout the circulatory system. The heart beats as an involuntary organ. We don't make a conscious decision to make it do what it does.

But to make a moral decision requires some kind of consciousness, an understanding of the moral issues or options involved so that the mind is intimately engaged in the choices that we make. As Christians, or as human beings, we can't assume that our ethical decisions, our moral responses, are mindless acts; rather, our actions result from the choices we make, which are informed by our thinking and formed by our minds. Scripture exhorts us to have the renewing of the mind so that we will begin to think in categories that God is pleased with, that our thinking will influence our choices, and that our choices will be in conformity to the law of God rather than in disobedience to them. The mind is vital to the Christian life.

A contrary view that is becoming more and more popular is physical determinism. In the twentieth century, psychologist B.F. Skinner concluded that all our responses are determined not only by our environment but also by our physical makeup. In the nineteenth century, Ludwig Feuerbach was famous for saying, "You are what you eat," noting that what people ingested for food had a profound impact on their biochemistry, and their biochemistry tended to determine their behavior. And in our law courts, we wonder whether people can be held accountable for their behavior, because if every decision is determined by one's environment or biochemical makeup, then how can anyone be held responsible for his actions?

What can we say to those who argue, as Skinner did, that everything we think is controlled and determined by physical causes? That kind of argument falls by its own weight. Anything, for example, that Skinner says about the nature of the mind and the nature of volition is itself conditioned by Skinner's biochemical composition and his background. And so his ideas have no more credence than anyone else's ideas. His theory eliminates cogency from the very act of thinking.

We will continue to explore what it means to have a Christian mind and how the mind is intimately involved in the Christian life in the chapters to come.

Chapter Two

Mind
and Body

We're always interested in frontier exploration. Some of the most thrilling adventure stories of the past are about people who risked life and limb to explore new areas of this planet. Today, we talk differently about the new frontier. Some think of outer space as being the dominant frontier of our day. Others are saying that the oceans are a brand-new frontier because we're just beginning to have the technology to explore their depths. But other scientists argue that the greatest and most significant frontier of our day is the human brain.

Think of the manifold ways that the brain records every word that we hear, every sight that we view, every experience that we have, and all the data that is stored in the brain.

Studies were made of professional athletes and of world-class concert pianists. A quarterback has to make countless decisions from the time he receives the snap from center, drops back to pass, reads the defense, sees his receivers, raises his arm, takes his arm back, brings it forward, and releases the ball. All these things transpire in a few seconds of action.

World-class piano players were also studied. They seem to have flying fingers, playing difficult passages of music with astonishing speed and accuracy. And what experts discovered in this brain research is that actual physiological changes take place in the brain, in the synapses, in the connecting tissue of the brain, which occur because of repetition. Athletes speak about "muscle memory." But memory is in the brain.

When someone asks a great golfer, "How did you hit that magnificent shot?" he might answer: "Well, my pre-shot routine is that I look at the flag and the green. I block out all the obstacles from my thinking—the sand traps, the water hazards—and then before I hit the shot, I visualize the kind of shot that I want to hit to the green, and then I just hit it." Great golfers talk about being in the zone, how all of a sudden the green looks huge and the pin looks a mile high and the cup five feet wide, and they have this visualization that sounds like some kind of Eastern mysticism, some Zen Buddhist approach to playing golf. They advise you to get the negative thoughts out of your mind and embrace the power of positive thinking.

If you're an amateur golfer, you have probably stood over your ball, looked at the green, and faced a lake between your ball and the green. And the last thing you probably thought before you took the club back was, "Don't hit it in the water." And so, what happened? You proceeded to hit it in the water. Why? Because the shot you hit into the water is a shot that you know how to make. Your brain knows how to hit that shot, and you called upon that with your thinking. People say that's negative visualization.

Is this some kind of mysticism? No. Scientists understand that there is a physiological dimension that relates to physical activity, connecting the brain and bodily reactions.

Now these things have nothing particularly to do with the Christian mind except that we as Christians can step back and look in astonishment at how fearfully and wonderfully we are made. What an enormous resource God has given His creatures with the brain. So far we've looked at physical relationships, because we don't live merely as thinkers. We play football, we play the piano, we play golf, we walk across the street, we ride bicycles—we are engaged in physical activity all the time because not only do we have a mind, but we also have a body.

Someone once asked me whether a feeling can create a thought, or does the thought create the feeling? My basic answer to that question is yes. It can go both ways, and we don't have to be neurological researchers to understand that. We experience that all the time. Think about it. You have a physical sensation in your stomach that you call a hunger pain. And as a result of that feeling, what happens? What thought goes through your mind? "I'd like to have some lunch now." In this case, your thinking is a response to your physical feeling.

On the other hand, if you're sitting and thinking about what you have to do tomorrow, and you think about all the things that can go wrong, then before you know it, you start feeling butterflies in your stomach or a pain in your head. Your body is responding physically to your thinking. This is what we call "psychosomatic interaction"; there is an interaction between the mind and the body.

As I've said, some people want to understand the mind as if it were totally disconnected from the body, and others want to explain thinking and the mind as if they were nothing more than a physical response. Christianity rejects both of those options. We believe that a powerful interplay exists between thought and action, between thought and feeling.

In the seventeenth century, with the advent and birth of the age of rationalism, the French mathematician René Descartes was absorbed with a question of causality: How are thought and action connected or related? How can I think about picking up the chair in front of me and then proceed to pick it up? Or conversely, how do physical actions produce or stimulate thinking?

This is not a simple matter because we think of the physical, or the material, as made up of quantitative things. We think of a fundamental distinction between the physical and the mental. They may be connected, they may be related, but they are not the same thing. A thought cannot be weighed. It takes up no space. It cannot be measured. It is nonphysical. And so we make a distinction between matter and thought, even though we understand that they can be related to each other. A thought can produce a material response, and a material response can produce a thought.

This is what Descartes was wrestling with as a philosopher-mathematician, and he developed a theory called interactionism. He said that there is some kind of interaction between thought and matter, between mind and body. But in trying to determine how a thought translates into an action, Descartes made a distinction between what he called "extension" and "nonextension." He made the distinction to indicate the difference between matter and mind. That which is physical always has some degree of extension. It takes up space and has weight. That which is mental has no weight, no size.

So how can you get from one realm to the other realm? That's one of the greatest mysteries about human life. Descartes theorized that the point of transition between thought and action is in the pineal gland at the base of the brain. His argument was based on mathematics. He said, "There has to be a point of transition between extension and nonextension." He liked the word *point* because, theoretically, you can have an infinite number of points on a line because a point takes up space but has no dimensions. It's neither fish nor fowl. It's neither pure extension or pure nonextension. Descartes was looking for a complicated category so that he could say, "There is the place where the transition takes place." But in truth, to this day we still don't know how this interaction takes place.

And it's because we don't know how this transition takes place that some try to deny that it takes place at all. But we know that there is a difference between our body and our mind. We know that we are responsible for our thinking and that our actions are intimately related to our thinking. It didn't take Descartes or modern neurological research to understand that as a man thinks in his heart, so is he (Prov. 23:7). We live out, in our physical lives, the deepest thoughts of our own minds. That's why we need transformed minds to have transformed lives.

Chapter Three

How Do You Know?

I once saw a bumper sticker that read, "I am a golfer; therefore I lie." This humorous bumper sticker was a takeoff of a famous phrase that originated with René Descartes, whom we have been looking at briefly. Descartes' famous formula was *cogito ergo sum*: "I think; therefore I am." Now, you might ask, Why would a philosopher spend any time or effort trying to prove his own existence? Why would a man like Descartes labor to establish this particular proposition?

A somewhat esoteric school of philosophy called solipsism rears its head periodically throughout Western history. Solipsism is the idea that all reality is an illusion or a projection of our own imagination. It raises the philosophical question, How do I know, for example, that you are real and not simply a figment of my imagination or a character in one of my dreams? And it gets even more bizarre when we ask the question, How do I know I'm not a character in one of your dreams? We know that sometimes our dreams can be so intense and graphic that after we awake, we're not sure whether what we have dreamed was real or imagined. Some philosophers have proposed that you can't be sure of your own personal existence.

Today we frequently hear the idea that we are living in the age of relativism and that there is no such thing as objective or absolute truth. We are told by relativism that truth is subjective or simply a matter of one's personal preference and that there is no such thing as fact or objective reality.

Such an assertion is devastating to historic Christianity because Christianity is based on certain propositions that we believe to be absolutely true, such as the existence of God and the truth claims of the New Testament. We do not say that the resurrection of Christ was a subjective experience that you can take or leave according to your own personal preferences, but we see it as an objective reality that demands a response from every human being.

But when you live in a culture where people say there is no such thing as truth, or there is no such thing as objectivity, and nothing can be known with any degree of certitude, someone like Descartes steps in to try to demonstrate at least one premise that is indubitable, that can be objectively and demonstrably proven. Of course, Descartes did not live in the twenty-first century. He lived in the seventeenth century, and he is generally considered the chief spokesman of the school of rationalism, which arose and dominated Western thought at that time.

The grand upheaval in the world of thought in the century before Descartes' life was the Protestant Reformation of the 1500s. The sixteenth-century Reformation, apart from its disputes about justification and the authority of the Bible and so on, had a tremendous impact on the shape of society as it contributed to the collapse of Christian unity and the monolithic authority of the church.

From early centuries and on through the Middle Ages, a particular axiom developed within the life of the church that was captured in a little Latin phrase: *fides implicitum*. Perhaps you've heard people say, "I want you to trust me implicitly." What does that mean? It means I want you to trust me without question, without rancor, without a rebellious spirit. You must acquiesce to my authority as a teacher, and I want you to believe what I say because I said so. This is the kind of thing parents do to their children after they get weary of answering their "why" questions. Parents patiently try to explain the reasons for their decisions, but after the sixth or seventh "why," they finally resort to "Because I said so." At that point, parents are asking for a surrender or an acquiescence of the child that he or she would simply take their word for something.

It may seem extremely arrogant for a church to expect its people to acquiesce through an implicit faith to whatever is taught by the church. But though the infallibility of the church was not defined until 1870, the idea was already in place. Now if, indeed, the church is infallible when it teaches things *de fide*, if the church has the grace of God that renders its teachings infallible, then would it not be entirely appropriate for a person to acquiesce implicitly?

Let's consider the idea outside the realm of the church, which we see as marred with the corruption of humanness, and let's turn our focus to God. Would a rational, thinking person simply render an implicit faith to anything uttered by almighty God? Or would you say: "I don't care who You are, O Creator. I want to see Your credentials"? When God shows His credentials, you know that it is God, and you know that this God is omniscient and eternal. If you encountered a being that you were convinced was eternal and knew everything and was all-righteous, and He made a proposition to you, would you believe it?

To give anything less than a *fides implicitum* to God would be arrogant. If we knew that it was God who was speaking, what creature would have any right to challenge the truthfulness of what comes from the mouth of God? So it is not a matter of blind faith for the Christian to place his trust in the living God when God speaks about things that we cannot fathom by our own naked intellect. That's why sometimes people get the idea that faith, as it manifests itself in the Christian life, is something gratuitous or irrational that reflects a psychological weakness in us, and that the only way we can affirm the existence of anything is by having immediate, demonstrative proof of it.

What Descartes was getting at is this: If we can establish the objective existence of God, then His very existence influences how we interpret everything in the universe. If you see a plant growing or a process taking place in a laboratory and you know that there is no God, how you understand the significance of the growth of that plant or the progress of that particular activity will be radically conditioned by that axiom that there is no God. On the other hand, if you know that there is a God who is transcendent and eternal and the Creator of all things and that He governs all things that come to pass, then your understanding of the plant—your understanding of life itself—is radically changed. That's why every person's worldview is either theocentric—that is, God-centered—or anthropocentric, man-centered. There is no more important premise than the premise of the existence of God.

If we understand that God exists and that He is eternal and omniscient, and if we can come to the conviction that the Scripture is His Word, then would it be irrational to acquiesce to the teaching of Scripture? If it is true that this is His Word, and, as Jesus proclaimed, "His Word is truth," wouldn't we be insane not to acquiesce to every word that proceeds from His mouth?

Of course, the great controversy is, Is it His Word? I understand the burden of Christian apologetics to give evidence that it is the Word of God. But again, if you are convinced on objective grounds that it is the Word of God, how foolish would it be to attack the truthfulness of what it says. If it's the Word of God, then it must be true, and if it's true, you are to acquiesce to it.

But in the sixteenth century, after the collapse of the unity of the church and the authority of the pope and the church councils, people were wrestling with this concept of an implicit faith in the teaching of the church. People still believed in putting their faith implicitly in God, but the question was, What does God say, and what does it mean? The best minds of the church in the sixteenth century were in great conflict over crucial theological affirmations.

As we transitioned into the seventeenth century, the basic question was, How can I know what is true? And suddenly, philosophy takes a new hard look at the question of epistemology. Epistemology is the study of the simple questions: How do we know what we know? How do we come to beliefs that we hold? Are they gratuitous, are they grounded in nothing, or is there some kind of objective basis for the truths that we affirm?

It was as if the church had to start all over again, and Western philosophy had to start all over again, asking the question that Pontius Pilate asked Jesus at His trial: "What is truth?" (John 18:38). And not only "What is truth?" but also "How can I know it?" Some people became cynical and said truth is unknowable. We can't know anything with certainty. It's into that situation that Descartes entered.

We've been told from ancient times that the unexamined life is not worth living, and I agree with that. And yet, I find it difficult to find many people who put their own philosophies and religious convictions under a microscope and ask: "Why do I believe what I believe? Do I believe it simply because it's been passed on to me by my parents or the subcultural community that I've been in?"

Why do you believe what you believe? What you believe determines how you live. It's a very important question to ask yourself, particularly as a Christian, because there is a real sense in which we are called to justify our belief systems, not just to our neighbor but to ourselves, because we are called to be mature in our faith. Paul tells us to be babes in evil but in our understanding to be adults (1 Cor. 14:20), which means we have to use the minds that God has given us to see the basis for our truth. This should not threaten us; it should encourage us. The more carefully we examine the data of Scripture, the more amazed we will be at the internal harmony and profundity of it.

Chapter Four

The Mind
and the Senses

We've been looking at some of the foundational issues of knowledge that preoccupied Christian thinkers and philosophers in the seventeenth century. Specifically, we have been examining the work of the French Jesuit mathematician René Descartes, who is famous for his slogan *cogito ergo sum*: "I think; therefore I am."

We considered why a man of the intellectual magnitude of Descartes would spend so much time trying to prove his own existence. As a result of the problems of the breakdown of authority, particularly in the church in the sixteenth century, these were the questions in the seventeenth century: How can I know if anything is true? How can I trust whatever knowledge I have received from my teachers, from the experts in various fields? This was a time when careful scrutiny was given to the science of epistemology, which studies the question, How can I know anything?

Descartes began his intellectual pilgrimage by declaring war on gratuitous assumptions. He said: "I am going to doubt everything that I have ever learned. I am going to doubt everything that I can conceivably doubt. I'm not going to take anything for granted."

Now, there still were a few things he took for granted, things he did not totally abandon, but his process was rigorous and systematic. He approached everything like this: "How can I know anything for sure about what I observe with my eyes or hear with my ears or taste with my mouth? How can I be certain of anything that I perceive with my senses?"

Today, our culture tends to say that unless we perceive it with the senses, we can have no confidence in its truthfulness at all. We say, "I want to see it, taste it, touch it, smell it," and so on. We want physical, tangible, sensible evidence to believe whatever it is that we believe. But Descartes said, "I'm going to challenge my very ability to perceive."

He challenged this on two separate levels. On the one hand, Descartes focused on what we call the subject-object problem (we'll look at the other problem in the next chapter). You as a living, breathing, thinking person are a "subject," and everything that exists outside of you could be called "objects." You're looking at me. I'm an object of your knowledge. And even though in myself I am a subject, as I look at you, you're an object of my perception.

The question in the subject-object problem is, How can I know for sure that the external world, the objective world, the world that exists outside of my own mind, really exists as I perceive it? This is no small question. We're asking, How accurate is my perception of reality? Is everything the way it seems to be as I perceive it, or is there some kind of built-in distortion that takes place in this transition between the external world and my mind? My ideas are in my mind, and my ideas about you are not gained by having a direct link-up between my mind and your mind. The only way I can get into your mind is if you choose to tell me something or reveal something about what's in your mind. And you do that in various ways. You may act it out. You may speak it. You may write it. But for me to get in touch with that, I have to use one or more of my five senses. I have to read with my eyes or hear with my ears, or, if I were blind, I could read it with my fingers with braille, but some part of my body would have to be engaged in this communication process between us. You see, the body is your personal transition to the world around you. Your way of getting from your mind to the external world is your body.

This was understood clearly by the writers of the sacred Scriptures. Peter, for example, said, "For we did not follow cleverly devised myths." That is, we're not writing fiction, things we've made up out of our own speculative imagination. "We made known to you the power and coming of our Lord Jesus Christ, but we were eyewitnesses of his majesty" (2 Peter 1:16). Or we think of doubting Thomas after the resurrection saying, "Unless I see in his hands the mark of the nails, and place my finger into the mark of the nails, and place my hand into his side, I will never believe" (John 20:25). Thomas was asking for what we call today empirical verification—that is, proof or evidence that is founded on sense perception, on seeing, tasting, touching, hearing, and so on, so that the mind (according to this theory) should not adopt or embrace as true that which cannot be verified or proven by the five senses.

Descartes turns the tables because of this problem of the subject and the object. Descartes said that sense perception is not the highest form of proof or the preferred method of arriving at certainty; he said it is an inferior way of getting at truth. He was not decrying or denying the utility of sensation, but he was trying to show the limits of learning truth simply through the senses. Because, again, how do you know that when you are seeing something, your eyes aren't playing tricks on you? What about a mirage or a hallucination?

A fascinating debate in the twentieth century took place at Harvard when Timothy Leary was performing experiments in the psychology department with hallucinogenic drugs. It was discovered that he was introducing a chemical substance called LSD into these experiments, and he got into trouble. There was a court trial about this case because it was against the law to be practicing this profession with the use of hallucinogenic drugs.

For his defense, Leary popularized the word *psychedelic*. Leary said that when one is under the influence of the mind-altering drug LSD, it is not that the mind's apprehension of reality is distorted, as is in the case of a hallucinogenic drug, but rather that the mind is enhanced. In other words, he was saying that LSD gives you a more accurate picture of what's actually out there than you have without the benefit of LSD. Artists and musicians testified that they saw blends and harmonies and hues and tints that they had never before been able to perceive with such acuity.

But what we're interested in, from an epistemological perspective, is this: Who can prove Leary wrong? How do you know that reality is as you perceive it? We do know, for example, that there are built-in limits to our sense perception.

We know that some animals have far more developed and acute senses than we do. For example, some animals have a far more advanced olfactory sense than we do. They can detect and track things that are miles away just by smell. Dogs can hear frequencies that we cannot—from a dog whistle, for example.

But Descartes would say: "How do you know that this isn't all one big distortion? How do you know that the lunatic in the insane asylum isn't having the accurate perception, and we are the ones that aren't perceiving reality truthfully?" Or suppose somebody else gets into the mix. How do you know that what you think you are seeing or hearing isn't a trick conjured up by the devil? Descartes would point to such things as the appearance of the medium of En-dor in the Old Testament, who conjured up Samuel for Saul (1 Sam. 28). Did the devil really have the ability to produce Samuel, or was it an illusion? How do you know? So Descartes considered the possibility of Satan as being the great deceiver, who went about causing people to come to a distorted knowledge of the truth.

Descartes went through a rigorous process of doubting everything that he could possibly doubt. Authorities disagree, so he couldn't appeal to authorities. How could he know anything for certain? He said: "There is one thing I cannot doubt without affirming at the same time that I'm doubting it, and that is I cannot doubt that I am doubting, because in order to doubt that I'm doubting requires that I doubt that I'm doubting. So that if I doubt that I'm doubting, I most certainly am doubting. And if I doubt it, I'm proving it."

The one thing he knew for sure was that he was doubting. And if he knew that for sure, then he knew something else: In order to doubt, doubt itself is some kind of thinking. It requires consciousness. It's not just a tingle in my toe, but it is a negative affirmation or denial in my head, in my thinking. So if I'm doubting, I must be thinking. Now, maybe I can doubt that I'm thinking, but in order to doubt that I'm thinking, I think. I must think that I'm not thinking. So even if I think that I'm not thinking, what am I doing? I'm thinking. So no matter how I come at this, I can't escape the indubitable truth that I'm thinking, and thought must have a thinker. And so Descartes said: "If I'm doubting, I'm thinking. If I'm thinking, I'm being. If I'm thinking, I am. I know that I'm thinking, *cogito*. I think; therefore I am."

But Descartes was not doing all this simply to prove to the world that René Descartes existed. What he was searching for was a starting point for the pathway to certainty, for the pathway to a truth that really matters for everybody. He was looking for a rational, intellectual foundation for affirming not the existence of Descartes but the existence of God.

Now, again, why would we go through such intellectual gymnastics to come to a conclusion that most of us just take uncritically and automatically as a given of our experience? Even the great Immanuel Kant did not try to prove the existence of the self. He referred to the transcendental apperception of the ego: You can't perceive yourself as a self. You can't see yourself, your innermost self, but you cannot deny it. It's integral to your own consciousness.

Descartes was trying to indicate that all thinking begins with consciousness. And so, from the Christian perspective, we have to ask, How does our consciousness include and relate not only to the consciousness we have of ourselves but also to our consciousness of God?

That is one of the most important questions a Christian will ever struggle with, and that is what we'll be looking at next.

Chapter Five

Two Ways
of Knowing

After René Descartes' rigorous doubt process, he came to his fundamental axiom "I think; therefore I am." The reason for this process was that Descartes was searching for certainty. He wanted to find some basis whereby he could know something for sure.

Much of what he wrestled with was the question of the degree of certainty that can be reached by two different avenues of investigative pursuit. There is the deductive approach or the formal approach to truth. Then there is the inductive approach or the material approach or, as it is sometimes more technically called in philosophy, the empirical approach. Empirical has to do with seeking knowledge by the senses.

Historically, the scientific method is a method that stands on two legs, the deductive and the inductive, or what we might call the formal and material, or the rational and the empirical. Sometimes we tend to think that the whole scientific enterprise is based purely on sense perception, the knowledge that we gain through the senses. The keen scientist is concerned with gathering data, studying behavioral patterns of various things in laboratories, and testing his theories with different experiments in order to verify his theories empirically—that is, on the basis of observable or measurable data or evidence. That is the inductive side of the scientific method.

The process of induction moves from the particular to the universal, or from bits of data to laws. We can observe and record our observations, particular incidents, or examples of something. We may, for example, look at ten squirrels and see that all ten have bushy tails. Then we may expand our study to a hundred squirrels, and we see that all one hundred have bushy tails, and we may expand to a thousand or to a hundred thousand squirrels, and we find one hundred thousand bushy tails. Soon we acquire enough data to make the assumption that bushy-tailedness is an integral part of squirrelness, so then we make a law that all squirrels have bushy tails.

But we have a couple of problems with that. The first problem we run into is the squirrel that got run over by a lawn mower and lost his bushy tail or one that has some kind of genetic deficiency and is born without a bushy tail. But beyond those anomalies, we have the other problem of finite investigation. No person has ever had the opportunity to study every squirrel that is or has ever been, and so we can never have an exhaustive, comprehensive knowledge of all squirrels. Yet science doesn't wait until we can examine every conceivable particular before we universalize.

The benefit of induction to science is that it curbs wild speculation or theorizing. Someone might say, "I believe personally in the existence of poltergeists and little men made out of green trees who live on the other side of the moon." And I might say, "What evidence do you have for your poltergeist?" He'll say, "I saw one." Then we find fifteen other people who say they had experiences with poltergeists. So a team of scientists studies this, and they find out that the evidence begins to evaporate. And then the person says: "But my poltergeists have a peculiar quality to them. They're allergic to scientists and to all kind of scientific equipment. So they always disappear at the first sight of an incoming scientist." That is suspect indeed.

Again, we could say that induction is the very heart and soul of modern scientific research. It is the gathering of the data. It is making careful observations and measurements, even using sophisticated equipment to examine the particulars so that we can learn a lot about the particulars as we look for general rules or laws. We realize that one of the goals of modern science is to be able to predict results. This is true for the application of particular medicines to different groups of people suffering different symptoms. We know that every individual in the world is to some degree unique, and not everybody is going to respond in the same exact manner to a particular medicine. But doctors make judgments based on inductive research.

The deductive side of the scientific method has to do with the conclusions you reach, or the inferences you make, from the data you collect and observe and do experiments with. Deduction has to do with the rational treatment of the data.

Science applies the rules of both deduction and induction and therefore states that the enterprise of knowing involves not only the senses but also the mind. And what we're calling the scientific method is not that different from the way the Scriptures speak. As we noted in the last chapter, the Bible refers to things that happen in the external, perceivable world. Peter said that they were not declaring cleverly devised myths that somebody could simply weave out of their own speculative imagination, but they were declaring those things that they had seen with their eyes and heard with their ears (see 2 Peter 1:16).

In other words, the Bible records narrative after narrative that make assertions about what people actually see or observe. That is, the resurrection of Jesus is not presented to us in the New Testament as a construction of fiction or as a theoretical, abstract possibility. The claim of the biblical writers is that an abundance of eyewitnesses testified to seeing Jesus die and, three days later, seeing Him come back from the grave so that much of the testimony of the Scriptures rests upon empirical observation.

But once we have observed something in the external, perceivable world, the obvious question is, So what? What is the significance of all this? What is the meaning of all this? That's where the mind is now actively engaged in trying to understand the import of the data.

Again, we see that the scientific method includes both of these elements. And on the surface, it appears that Descartes was eliminating half of it—namely, the inductive side, because he was going to doubt every single thing that he perceived. He said, "I never can know for sure that my senses are not deceiving me." That is the subject-object problem we considered in the previous chapter.

The other problem is that we never can have absolute certainty about anything from the senses. Does that mean I cannot have absolute certainty about the truth of something that I see with my own eyes? What about "seeing is believing"? If I were standing in front of the tomb on Easter morning and saw Jesus come out of that grave and in His resurrected state, wouldn't I be absolutely convinced of His resurrection?

We certainly put a lot of weight on what we can see with our own eyes or hear with our own ears. Over the years of our personal experiences, we have come to the place where we invest a lot of credibility in our own particular experiences—that is, not just what we're feeling, but what we're actually observing or actually hearing with our own ears.

When I talk about absolute certainty, I use that term in the philosophical sense. Absolute certainty refers to that which cannot rationally be questioned. But we know that eyewitnesses can be wrong and that not all eyewitness testimony is infallible; people think they see things that aren't really there. Now, if a hundred thousand people agree completely on seeing a given event on a particular day, it's extremely unlikely that all one hundred thousand of them were undergoing an illusion or a hallucination. But theoretically, is it possible that a hundred thousand people at the same time have a hallucination? Yes, though again, it's extremely unlikely.

We run into this problem of evidence in the courtroom, particularly when we talk about reasonable doubt. In criminal cases, it is the burden of the prosecution to prove its case beyond a reasonable doubt. That's not the same thing as beyond a shadow of a doubt. You can raise doubts about anything if you want to, except that you are doubting, because the doubt that you were doubting proves that you were doubting. But this was what Descartes was trying to explain. He said there are built-in limitations to the empirical side of knowledge. We never can have absolute certainty from our senses.

Well, is there anywhere we can have absolute certainty? Descartes said yes, in the formal realm, in the deductive realm. In the rational realm, we can have absolute, rational certainty. And that takes us to the standard syllogism: "All men are mortal. Socrates is a man. Therefore, Socrates is mortal."

Can we know the first premise, "All men are mortal," absolutely? No, because we haven't examined all men, have we? It may be that every human being who ever lived before this moment was mortal but that this generation of people is the first generation in history that is immortal. Now that's highly unlikely, but the only way you can know with absolute philosophical certainty that all men are mortal is posthumously—that is, if everybody died.

But we assume, on the basis of the data and the extreme probability, that all men are mortal and that Socrates was a man. Maybe Socrates was a figment of Plato's imagination. Maybe Socrates was an alien from another planet. Those are wild, crazy possibilities, but we don't know for certain that Socrates was a man. But here's the value of the syllogism. If all men are mortal, if this premise is true, and if Socrates is a man, if that premise is true, then we know with absolute certainty that Socrates was mortal.

This deductive side, the formal side, gives us the certainty of an absolute conclusion that is proven demonstratively from the premises. That becomes crucial not only for natural science but also for theological science, as we will see.

My purpose is not to create skepticism in your mind about what you see and hear and experience. I believe and assume, for example, that the senses I use to observe and to hear what's going on around me, though they are not perfect and though they are not infallible, nevertheless are reliable. And I believe I'm morally responsible to act according to the perceptions that I have.

We don't want to be adrift in a sea of cynical skepticism about science or about sense perception. This is how we are constructed as creatures. As we saw earlier, the only transition, the only portal, from our mind to the world outside of the mind is through the senses. And so, I put great weight on sense perception, as the Bible does and as science does. We must remember, however, that our sense perception has limits.

Chapter Six

The Laws of Logic

As we continue with our study of the Christian and the mind, I want to make some further observations about the significance of the work of Descartes in the seventeenth century. We recall that after his rigorous process of doubting everything that he could conceivably doubt, he concluded, "I think; therefore I am." In order to doubt, he reasoned, I have to be thinking. And in order to be thinking, I have to exist. And if I doubt that I'm thinking, I have to think in order to be doubting. To doubt that I'm doubting requires that I'm doubting that I'm doubting. So no matter how I slice it, I can't escape the conclusion that I am doubting, and if doubting, thinking, and if thinking, being.

Now Descartes wanted to get to the bottom line of certainty, where he wasn't assuming anything that couldn't be challenged. But for him to be absolutely certain that to think means that he exists, he has to assume two principles, both of which are closely related to each other.

The first is the law of noncontradiction. This law states that *A* cannot be *A* and non-*A* at the same time and in the same relationship. That is to say, a thing or a proposition cannot be what it is and not be what it is at the same time and in the same relationship. We use the symbols *A* and non-*A* as a kind of philosophical shorthand.

A person *can* be *A* and *B* at the same time. I can be a father and a son at the same time—but not in the same relationship. Now, when Descartes says, "I think; therefore I am," he assumes the law of noncontradiction. He is assuming that if he is thinking, he is not at the same time, in the same way *not* thinking. You can't think and non-think at the same time and in the same relationship. You cannot doubt and not be doubting at the same time in the same relationship. And so he assumes the validity of a rational principle or a rational law, a rational form of thinking. That's why we call this a formal principle.

The second principle Descartes assumes is the law of causality, because when he says, "I think; therefore I am," he's assuming that thought requires a thinker or that doubt requires a doubter. That is, thought is something that occurs that requires an antecedent cause for it. Something has to cause that thought; something has to cause that doubt. Descartes would say that it is his own existence.

People today may think that Descartes was naive in the seventeenth century to assume such a principle as the law of causality because now we know that in the next century, Scottish philosopher David Hume would present a comprehensive critique of causality. People today, unfortunately, can rest at ease that we no longer have to assume the validity of the law of causality.

In my book *Not a Chance*, I engage with people of the past, most notably Bertrand Russell. In his book *Why I Am Not a Christian*, Russell argued that he was persuaded as a young man that he couldn't escape the logical necessity of affirming the existence of God because he figured that if something exists now, something has to cause it. The old causal argument for the existence of God persuaded Russell as a child that God must necessarily exist.

Then, when he was a teenager, he read an essay written by John Stuart Mill in which Mill objected to the classic argument for the existence of God. Mill said that argument rests on the concept of the law of causality. But if the law of causality is true and everything must have a cause, then manifestly, God must have a cause. So there is no rational necessity for deducing the existence of God from the existence of anything else, because if everything requires a cause, then God would require a cause, and whatever caused God would require a cause, and we would go on *ad infinitum* (infinite regress).

But John Stuart Mill made a fundamental error. And Mill's error persuaded Russell when Russell was eighteen years old, and Russell never recovered from this erroneous conclusion of his mentor.

The problem is simple. They were operating on a false, inaccurate, and invalid definition of the law of causality. The law of causality does not affirm that everything must have a cause. What the law of causality affirms is much simpler than that; it is that every effect must have a cause. Do you see the difference? If I say that *anything that is* must have a cause, and that applies to God and everything else, we are left with the nonsense of an infinite regress.

But if you say that every *effect* must have a cause, suddenly the value of the principle of causality is diminished because the statement "every effect must have a cause" is what we call a formal truth or an analytical truth. Or, to make it simpler, it is a statement that is true by definition; it is true by the sheer power of its internal logic. Because an effect, to be an effect, is something that has a cause. That is, the definition of an effect is that which has a cause. And the definition of a cause is that which produces an effect. So if there are no effects, there can be no causes. If there are no causes, there can be no effects. However, conversely, if there is an effect, then it must have a cause. And if there's a cause, it must yield an effect. An effect without a cause is not an effect, and a cause without an effect is not a cause.

In the book I coauthored with John Gerstner and Arthur Lindsley, *Christian Apologetics*, I mention causality. And in a review in a technical journal, a Christian philosopher made one objection to my reasoning. He said that the problem with Sproul is that Sproul will not allow for an uncaused effect. And I responded to him briefly, saying: "You've got me. You're absolutely right. Sproul will not allow for an uncaused effect. But you cite this as a problem, and I thought it was a virtue."

I said that I was willing to retreat from my assertion that there's no such thing as an uncaused effect if he could give one example from nature or history of an uncaused effect. As soon as he saw what he had said, he realized that an uncaused effect is a nonsense statement. It is formally impossible. It is manifestly illogical.

When we understand the law of causality as properly stated "for every effect, there is an antecedent cause," we see that this law is simply an extension of the law of non-contradiction; it rests on the assumption that that which is an effect cannot *be* an effect and *not be* an effect at the same time and in the same relationship. And that which is a cause cannot be a cause and not be a cause at the same time and in the same relationship.

Now, we're talking about the elementary principles of thinking and knowledge, and of getting intellectual clarity about things. Descartes didn't labor the point of these assumptions because not only did Descartes assume the validity of the law of noncontradiction, but he also understood it to be a necessary assumption for anybody's thinking about anything in a discursive way.

Every time I talk about the law of noncontradiction, someone in the Christian community objects: "R.C., aren't you bringing into Christian faith a pagan idea that Aristotle invented? Isn't Aristotle the father of the first classic structure of systems of logic? And isn't there a great distance between the thinking of the Jew in the Old Testament and the abstract, logical, relentless, deductive approach to things that we find in classical Greek philosophy? Isn't this just one more example of the intrusion of a pagan idea into Christian thought?"

My response is, I think you're giving Aristotle far too much credit here and me, conversely, too much blame, because I don't believe that Aristotle invented logic or created logic any more than I believe that Columbus invented the Americas or created the Americas. What Columbus did was discover something that was already there. And all that Aristotle was trying to do was to define rules of thought that were already built into rationality, into creatures who have minds.

We know that Aristotle was a prolific writer and that the scope of his intellectual pursuits was vast. He examined arenas of ethics, aesthetics, physics, biology, philosophy, and a host of others. He would distinguish among these as pursuits of various sciences. But he did not consider logic to be a science. Rather, he called logic the *organon* of all science. We translate the Greek *organon* as "instrument" or "tool." Aristotle said that logic is merely a tool a person who is seeking understanding and knowledge in all these other spheres uses.

He said that logic is not only a tool or an instrument of thought but a necessary tool for intelligible discourse. That is, logic is necessary for us to be able to speak to one another in an intelligible way.

Many years ago I taught a senior class of seminarians in philosophical theology. When teaching the philosopher Immanuel Kant, we discussed the nature of truth and of propositions. As I held up a piece of chalk, I asked my students: "What kind of a proposition is this? *This piece of chalk is not a piece of chalk.* What have you learned from that? What do I mean when I say, 'This piece of chalk is not a piece of chalk'?"

The valedictorian of the class said, "What you mean is that particular piece of chalk that you have in your hand is not really a piece of chalk." And I said, "Which piece of chalk?" He said, "The particular piece of chalk that you have in your hand." I said: "But that's exactly the particular piece of chalk that I'm talking about. This particular piece of chalk is not a piece of chalk." Then he said, "I don't know what you mean, then."

The dean of the institution was visiting the class that day, so I asked him: "Dean, can you help us out? The students don't understand the significance and the meaning of the statement 'This piece of chalk is not a piece of chalk.' What do I mean by that?" The dean said, "What you're talking about has to do with substance and accidents, the old metaphysical problem. You're saying that the piece of chalk that you're holding may have the accidents of chalk-iness, but it lacks the substance of chalkiness." I replied: "But I'm not talking about the accidental piece of chalk here. I'm stating that the essential chalk that I have here in my hand is not essential chalkiness." He said, "Well then, I don't know."

I could see that one student in the class was getting more and more disgusted with this discussion. I asked him what he thought of the discussion. He said, "What you're saying here is a nonsense statement." And I said, "Thank You, Lord; we have one sentient creature left in this classroom." In other words, this man not only was educated, but he knew how people play games with words, and he recognized it for what it was. Anyone armed with the law of noncontradiction should have recognized it immediately as a violation of the law of noncontradiction, and as a nonsense statement. My statement was unintelligible to any rational mind.

But you see, my students had more trust in me than to think that I would deceive them. They were looking for something more profound, something deeper. But I was trying to teach them that no matter how many degrees you have after your name, a contradiction is still a contradiction, and it's a nonsense statement, and no matter how much education you have, you don't have the authority to carry the day with nonsense statements. That's part and parcel of what Descartes concluded. In the next chapter, we will see how this all fits together with respect to Descartes' argument for the reality of God.

Discussions on the laws of logic can seem difficult and abstract, but all we're talking about here are the basics of thinking and of speaking in a manner so that, as people talk together, we can have meaningful discussions.

I know it can all sound abstract. But so often, we get off

base in our thinking, philosophy, and theology at the very beginning, on the basic foundational issues of knowledge. And from time to time, we need to go back to the basics, back to what we would call the foundational principles of truth.

Chapter Seven

Rationality and Rationalism

In our time spent with philosopher René Descartes, we've wondered why someone would go through such intellectual gymnastics just to come to the conclusion of his own existence. The answer is that Descartes wanted to establish grounds for the central affirmation of the Christian faith: the existence of God.

We must also understand that Descartes was perhaps as famous in his day for his work in the field of mathematics as he was as a philosopher. Many of the most incredible advances in modern science have often been spearheaded by the work of mathematicians.

For example, Copernicus challenged the idea of geocentricity—namely, that the earth is the center of the universe, or at least the center of the solar system. He challenged the idea that the sun revolves around a fixed center in the solar system, and that fixed center is the earth. Copernicus worked to annihilate ancient assumptions that had been worked out in a convoluted mathematical way by the Ptolemaic philosophers of antiquity. He replaced geocentricity with heliocentricity—that is, the sun is the center of the solar system and the planets are moving around the sun.

We have a hard time today grasping how radical that was. The bishops of the church refused to look into Galileo's telescope and ultimately condemned Galileo when he sought to confirm the Copernican theory with empirical evidence. They assumed that the Bible taught that the earth was the center of the universe because the language of the Bible describes the sun as moving across the sky. From where we stand when we look up at the sky, it appears as if we are stationary and the sun is moving across the horizon. It rises in the east and sets in the west.

Not only that, but if someone in the thirteenth century said, "We are standing on a surface that is spinning around in a circle, and the world is round, and it's turning around," you would ask, "Then why haven't I fallen off?" Centrifugal force and centripetal force were unknown to people in those days, and so they made their judgments about the world around them chiefly on the basis of what they could see.

So why would Copernicus challenge something that was so deeply rooted in scientific and philosophical tradition and deeply established in terms of a person's normal experience? The key to understanding the Copernican revolution is recognizing that some earlier astronomers were not satisfied with the cumbersome system of mathematics that was being used to make the predictions of the old science work out. It was the mathematicians who realized that they could simplify the complicated math if they consider the sun to be at the center and not earth.

Once they had fine-tuned the math, they began to see a proportionate ratio of the distances from the sun of the various planets in our solar system. Then later mathematicians used their calculations and worked out these complicated proportions and essentially said, "If our calculations are correct and this math works out in a consistent manner, then there should be another planet out here somewhere." When they pointed the telescope at that region of the sky (once the telescope was invented), they discovered another planet right where the math told them it would be. So, this great step forward in understanding our position in the vastness of this universe was stimulated initially by mathematicians.

And what about Newtonian physics? Isaac Newton was a master mathematician. What about in our own generation, what some describe as "the atomic age"? Atomic physics has revolutionized how we live and think and how we understand the universe in which we live. The genius behind that was Albert Einstein, who was a genius in the field of mathematics.

Now, what is math? It is not just arithmetic, but it is something that involves numbers. We learned in elementary mathematics that two plus two equals four. The first question I want to ask is, "Two *what* plus two *what* equals four *what*?" The answer is, "It doesn't matter." It can be bananas or kangaroos. If you have two bananas and you add to those two bananas two more bananas, how many bananas do you have? Four. And it's the same thing with kangaroos. So when we talk in simple, elementary math, we are not being concrete and specific about various entities like bananas and kangaroos. We simply reduce it to a mathematical formula. And this number *2* is a symbol, as is the number *4* and the = sign.

What we have in the formula 2 + 2 = 4 is a symbolic representation of what we call a *tautology*. A tautology is a statement where the predicate adds nothing new in terms of information to the subject. An example of a tautological statement is "A bachelor is an unmarried man." The whole idea of unmarried man-ness is already contained in the word *bachelor*. We don't get any new information when we use the predicate "unmarried man." There is a formal truth affirmed in the formula 2 + 2 = 4. To state it simply, mathematics is a sophisticated kind of symbolic logic. That is to say, the relationship of both sides of the equation is a *rational* relationship. If I say 2 + 3 = 4, I now have an irrational formula because it's incoherent; it violates the laws of logic. What mathematics does is apply logic and rationality systematically in a symbolic way.

I am laboring this point for a reason. In the seventeenth century a theory called conceptualism arose, which was an extreme form of the dominant movement of the seventeenth century known as rationalism. Conceptualism took the tenets of rationalism to an extreme. Adherents of conceptualism argued that anything that could be conceived of as internally coherent and logical must exist in reality. So, for instance, people searched the world for unicorns because they said, "A unicorn is not an animal that is inconceivable." And anything that could be conceived of rationally must necessarily exist in the real world. (This has to do with one of the classical arguments for the existence of God, which we will explore later.)

Looking at that from the vantage point of the twentieth century, we think, "That's silly." The mind has the ability to exercise abstraction, to extend categories. I look at various animals, and I see that lots of animals have legs, and in fact, almost all of them do. Then I see certain animals that have four legs, and I can conceive of a four-legged animal, a horse. I have an idea of horseness in my mind. But I also know of rhinoceroses, and they have a big horn right on the front of their nose. And so all I to do is transfer the idea of the horn from the rhinoceros and put it on the nose of the horse. And I have a unicorn. There is nothing irrational about the idea of a unicorn. There is no reason why unicorns couldn't exist. But who would say that just because we can doodle on a page and transfer body parts from one kind of animal to another, these animals therefore exist? For a very short period of time, people did believe that if you could conceive of it rationally, it must exist.

This reasoning came about because people began to have great confidence in mathematics. Since mathematics is a rational, logical science that formalizes concepts, and since mathematics had led to the discovery of all kinds of things, people's confidence in that particular discipline was highly elevated. Mathematics is a science that is inherently rational. When I look at our culture today and see how we have embraced the irrationality of Eastern religion and existential philosophy and relativism, I ask, "Who is going to save us from this immersion into absurdity?" I don't think it's going to be the philosophers, because they're enjoying it. And it probably won't be the theologians, because we've seen theology embrace irrationality. But the one place irrationality does not work is on the computer screen. If we're going to continue this explosion of technology, we can't throw away the fundamental, rational consistency of mathematics. I look to the scientists, the naturalists, to save us from this pervasive spirit of irrationality.

Again, we recall that Descartes was a mathematician before he was a philosopher. As the father of rationalism, he was looking for the kind of truth that is delivered by mathematics. The conclusion that 2 + 2 = 4 comes from a resistless logic; it is indubitable. (Those who say they can mathematically prove that 2 + 2 = 5 end up changing the meaning of terms, something we call the problem of equivocation.)

Descartes was looking for a clear and distinct idea whose truth was incapable of being doubted, a formal affirmation that was certain, from which he could then deduce all truth. We call this *a priori* thinking. *A priori* means "before experience." I don't have to experience something; I can know it by deduction, by sheer logical inference.

Descartes wanted to deduce the central truths of all reality, prior to experience, without having to see it, taste it, touch it, smell it, or hear it. And so that's the procedure he followed to try to establish the truth of the existence of God.

There is a reason that mathematics is stressed in the educational curriculum for the development of children. In this arena, more than any other, children's rational thinking processes are developed. They don't realize when they're studying math that they're actually studying a form of logic. They are studying a kind of symbolic logic, where the equations are abstract symbolic representations of certain actions and quantities. It is important for us to see that God has made us and the world we live in with a magnificent symmetry of mathematical proportionality. Key to our exploration of the world is the application of this science that makes use of the mind.

Chapter Eight

Faith
and Reason

One of the things I try to assert as a Christian teacher and apologist is that Christianity is rational. However much we embrace the reality and the importance of faith in our Christian experience, the faith that we are called to exhibit as Christians is not an irrational faith.

Some say that there's something virtuous about the Christian who takes a leap of faith that is against reason. But nowhere in the Bible does God call us to leap into the abyss of absurdity. We are not called to leap into the darkness; we're called to jump out of the darkness and into the light, and God is not an author of confusion. There is no virtue in affirming both poles of a contradiction, because to do so is to say that the author of truth speaks with a forked tongue.

Theologians of the early part of the twentieth century not only affirmed the possibility of contradiction within Christian truth but saw this as an important element of mature faith. Karl Barth, for example, in his *Epistle to the Romans*, stated that a Christian does not become mature until that person is able to affirm both poles of a contradiction. He called that maturity. I call it confusion. His comrade Emil Brunner wrote *Truth as Encounter*, in which he argued that truth is more than cold, abstract propositions, particularly Christian truth. Christian truth is concerned not with the logical coherence of propositions but with a personal relationship. Truth has a subjective element to it that is unmistakable. And that's true. We are concerned about a personal relationship, a subjective relationship between you as a subject and God as a subject. It's one thing to say that, but it's another thing to embrace what we call subjectivism, which says that truth is determined by you. Brunner argued (wrongly) that contradiction is the very hallmark of truth.

If contradiction is the hallmark of the truth, what happens when we apply that statement to the fall, when the serpent comes to Eve? God had said to Adam and Eve, "If you eat of this tree, you will surely die." If *A*, then *B* will inevitably follow. Then the serpent comes to Eve and says, "If you eat of the tree, you will not die, but you will become as gods."

If we translate that into logical propositions, what the serpent is saying is, "If *A*, non-*B*." When God says, "If *A*, then *B*" and the serpent says, "If *A*, then non-*B*," we have the first record of a blatant contradiction, right there in Genesis 3. And Eve bought it. This is the first act of human disobedience that plunges the whole world into ruin.

Now, let's apply the principle that contradiction is the hallmark of truth. Imagine that Eve, being astute, understood Brunner's principle that contradiction is the hallmark of truth, and that she wanted to be mature in her faith. She says: "I noticed this contradiction, but Brunner says that if I'm going to be mature in my faith, I have to be willing to embrace both poles of a contradiction. Not only that, but if Brunner is correct, then what I have just heard from this serpent is a contradiction, and that's the hallmark of truth. If contradiction is the hallmark of truth and God is the author of the truth, then what the serpent is saying to me must not only be the truth, but it must be the veritable truth of God. So now, not only may I eat of this fruit, but I have a moral obligation to do what the serpent says."

Suddenly, the fall is not a fall but one great step forward for mankind. I don't know how else we can be tested for our faith and practice if we have no way of discerning the difference between obedience and disobedience, between righteousness and unrighteousness, between Christ and the Antichrist, other than that these categories are contradictory.

When God says one thing and somebody else says that which contradicts it, we are now morally accountable to reject the contradiction. God has equipped us with these categories of thinking and applying sound principles of the mind to real-life situations. This is absolutely essential to being a Christian.

Why would someone be so enticed by existential philosophy and irrationality that he would not only hold contradictory truths to be integral to Christianity but also exult in them? To answer that, we have to go back to the Enlightenment of the eighteenth century. People at that time said, "If we're going to exalt reason to the level of significance that it alone can give us certitude, then we need a religion based on reason and reason alone." Now, reason is set over against another category that we call *revelation*.

The attempt was to establish religion without the Bible, without any dependence on special revelation and based purely on what's called "natural reason." That is, on the basis of sheer speculation, we can come to all the truth we ever need. Immanuel Kant wrote a book on this topic called *Religion within the Limits of Reason Alone*.

If we look at the last four or five hundred years of church history, we wonder what has happened that has caused the church to be virtually driven out of the mainline of human experience. For proof of this, you simply need to drive through the little villages and towns of New England. As you drive through those little towns, you'll notice that at the geographical center of every one is a church dating back to the Colonial period. This tells you that the church was at the center of the life of the people. It was the fundamental source and fountain of education and religion. Today, we have put the church geographically on the outer edge of our society. The laws of the country still protect your free exercise of religion, as long as it remains a private and personal matter and does nothing to intrude into the public square.

What we have seen is the triumph of naturalism over biblical supernaturalism, but with a certain genteel tolerance that is part of the legacy of earlier generations and earlier legislation that still allows us to exercise our irrational faith in our homes or in our churches—as long as we don't disturb anybody else with it. This triumph of naturalism was, in many ways, driven by an unreserved confidence in and commitment to natural reason that was cloaked in a movement called rationalism. This is why I run into problems in the church when I start pleading for people to remember that Christianity is rational. The fear that immediately emerges when I say that Christianity is rational is that people associate *rationality* with *rationalism*. Christianity manifestly rejects rationalism if what we mean by *rationalism* is that truth is discerned by the pure efforts of human reason without any dependence on divine revelation. Whatever else Christianity is, it is a revealed religion, and we are committed to submitting to truth that comes to us from the Word of God, truths that are never discerned or discovered simply by unaided natural reason.

The church has to resist any kind of naturalism or rationalism that seeks to supplant the authority of divine revelation. Once we enter the Christian faith and we firmly commit ourselves to submission to the revelation of God and are not willing to negotiate that Christianity is a revealed faith, we face these next questions: Is the revelation that God gives to us rational, as distinguished from irrational? Is the truth that God reveals intelligible? Is it coherent? Is it consistent internally? Or do we have a Bible in which one writer in the Bible flatly contradicts another writer in the Bible, but we say both of them are telling the truth? Assuming that God doesn't speak with a forked tongue and that the Holy Spirit is not the author of confusion, when we struggle with what James said on one hand and what Paul said in another context on another hand, do we simply say, "They just contradict each other"? Or, if we know that both of them are agents of revelation and both are instruments that God uses to reveal His truth— and knowing that God is not wicked in that He would lie to people—do we now say, "These texts deserve a second glance"? I may initially be jarred by the apparent conflict between passages, but if I look at them carefully and deeply, I will begin to see the internal harmony.

Over the last two hundred years, great scholars have pointed out all kinds of internal difficulties of harmonization in the written Scriptures. For the most part, higher critical scholarship has abandoned the classic Christian view of the inspiration of the Bible, arguing that only backwoods fundamentalists who have no education would still hold to this antiquated theory of divine inspiration.

We all acknowledge that if a book were written over a period of hundreds, indeed thousands, of years, by different authors in different cultures and different times, talking to different subjects, we would expect to find apparent discrepancies at the outset. But you don't just throw in the towel. You begin to examine it in greater depth. One thing higher criticism has done is force orthodox Christians to do their homework and go to the next level of biblical analysis. When I personally engage in this next level of analysis, I am overwhelmed by the internal consistency of the details of biblical Scripture.

The last thing William Foxwell Albright, who was to archaeology what Einstein was to physics, published was his preface to the Anchor Bible series of New Testament commentaries. He was angry, and he said there was no excuse for twentieth-century scholarship to continue to rest on highly questionable philosophical assumptions and ignore archaeology and objective standards of testing.

I remember reading that and thinking, "That's exactly where we are in biblical scholarship." We have gotten to this point, partly, because we've embraced irrationality. What Descartes was trying to show, and what I am trying to show, is that embracing Christianity is not the same as embracing rationalism. But Christianity is *rational*. It is not an exercise in absurdity.

To apply these things in a practical way, you can ask yourself: "What do I believe in terms of what the Bible teaches? Is there in my personal theology an instance where I find myself affirming both poles of a contradiction?" If you can say yes to that, then you should say, "If this is the Word of God, then somewhere along the line I have misunderstood it."

You see, what reason does for our minds is not construct an idol of gold, but reason acts like a police officer on the corner with a whistle, so that when you start running through the stop sign, the whistle blows. Rationality says: "Time out! You're confused. You've made a mistake. This does not compute." And rather than just throwing away the Bible in despair, you say, "If this doesn't compute, then there is something here I don't understand." Socrates understood that the beginning of learning is when you realize that you've run into a wall and cannot find clarity. That is God's way of saying: "Look at it more deeply. Look at it more broadly. Let's try to see if we can resolve this." Working with difficult texts can be quite edifying.

Chapter Nine

Two Kinds of Being

René Descartes had a great desire to find some truth that was indubitable. He wanted to find a rational foundation to argue for the existence of God. Now, the way Descartes argued for the existence of God differed from his predecessors. Frankly, I don't think his argument for the existence of God was as compelling as some of the earlier thinkers and even one who came after him. Descartes developed what we call an ontological argument.

Ontology is the science or the study of *being*. The ontological argument for the existence of God is related to the question of being. The most famous version of the ontological argument was produced much earlier than Descartes by Anselm of Canterbury. Anselm argued in this fashion. He began by saying, "God is that being than which no greater can be conceived." Some have tried to translate that into simple language by saying that Anselm defined God as "the most perfect conceivable being," but that's not quite accurate. He argued that not only must we think of God as a mental construct or as an idea, but we must also think of God as existing. If I conceive of God only as a hypothetical possibility, I am not thinking of Anselm's God because Anselm would say, "There is a higher conceivable being— namely, one that exists not only in the mind's conception but who exists in reality, because it is greater to exist than not to exist."

Anselm's argument is well known, but his is not the only way people have reasoned ontologically for the existence of God. In a way that's much easier to follow, the medieval philosophers and theologians argued that God is or has what is called necessary being, as distinguished from unnecessary being or contingent being.

There are two differences between a necessary being and a contingent being. One is a *logical* difference, and the other is an *ontological* difference. When we talk about necessary being, we are talking about a being that cannot *not* be. By the sheer power of its being, it cannot *not* exist. Now, the reason for that kind of distinction is to distinguish God from all creatures. You exist right now, but you don't have necessary being. It's very possible that you could not exist. In fact, there was a time when you did not exist. So, since there was a time when you did not exist, we cannot assert of your existence that it's necessary ontologically, because if you had to be by sheer necessity of the power of your own being, there never would have been a time that you did not exist.

But God's being is such that He is eternal. He has the power of being within Himself. And being a self-existent eternal being, He cannot not exist; that is, if God always existed from all eternity, we can safely assume that He will continue to exist because He is self-existent. His existence or His being is not dependent on anything outside Himself. Your existence, on the other hand, is dependent on water and food and the absence of certain diseases and so on. And your present existence depends on your having been born, on your having been generated at some point in time.

But God was not generated in some point of time, and God is not dependent on anything outside of Himself, like water or air or food, in order for Him to be. He has the power of being within Himself. That is what we mean by "ontologically necessary being."

But what we're concerned about more here is the second way that the phrase *necessary being* was used by the old philosophers and theologians. They said that the existence of God is not only ontologically necessary but also *logically* necessary; that is, it is a necessity of logic to affirm the existence of God, and if you deny the existence of God, you are being illogical or irrational. In other words, reason itself demands the existence of God, and to deny the existence of God is to step out of rationality.

Part of the reason why these ancient philosophers and theologians argued in this manner was to challenge people who were raising questions about the idea of God's existence based on sense perception. People would say: "No one has ever seen God. You can't taste Him, touch Him, or smell Him." That is, we have no sense perception of God, as we do with other forms of reality. Skeptics would say, "Since we cannot demonstrate the existence of God through external sensory evidence, then we ought not to affirm His existence at all." But the philosophers said that apart from the senses, reason requires as a logical necessity the idea of God.

Descartes was trying to give us a foundation on which to make that rational assertion because it is rationally conceivable for God not to exist if nothing exists. Even to say that nothing exists requires something of a slip of the tongue, because "nothing," by definition, does not exist. It is sheer nonexistence or sheer nonbeing.

But we can conceive theoretically of the idea of pure nothingness. We can affirm an object as existing, such as a person or a chair. We can say that neither the person nor the chair is necessary. I can consider the possibility that neither the person nor the chair exists because there was a time when neither the person nor the chair actually existed. So we say, "Not only can we conceive that the person didn't exist or doesn't exist, but we can conceive that nobody existed." There was a time when there weren't any people, and there was a time when there weren't any chairs, and there was a time when there weren't any oceans, and there was a time when there weren't any stars.

If there was a time when absolutely nothing existed, then what would there be now? The only thing you could have now would be nothing, unless you argued that at some point in the midst of this nothingness, something came into being by itself. It just popped into existence out of nothing—no material cause, no efficient cause, no sufficient cause, no power behind it, absolutely nothing. And then suddenly there is something. Some call it *spontaneous generation*, while others use the term *self-creation*.

The concept of self-creation is manifestly irrational, illogical, and absurd because it violates the most fundamental rule of logic—namely, the law of noncontradiction, which we looked at in the last chapter. For something to create itself, it has to be and not be at the same time and in the same relationship. To create itself, it would have to be before it was, which means that it would have to be there and not be there at the same time in the same relationship, which is irrational. It's absurd. This idea is, from a rational perspective, complete nonsense.

The rationalists, including Descartes, argued that if something exists now, then something must have always existed. That is, there never could have been a time when there was absolutely nothing. Something somewhere must have the power of being within itself for anything to be. That is, there must be a necessary being, a being who exists by his own internal necessity, and that necessary being not only exists by ontological necessity, but it is logically necessary that a necessary being exists.

It is logically necessary that an ontologically necessary being exists if something exists now, and this is what Descartes understood. This was the genius of his rigorous doubting process. Once he could prove the existence of anything indisputably, then he could come to the conclusion of the eternal self-existence of God. Descartes started with arguing that his own existence was indisputable because to dispute it is to affirm it. That's the importance of his formula "I think; therefore I am"; to deny that premise, one has to doubt it, and to doubt it requires thinking, and so to doubt it affirms the very proposition that is being doubted. So, Descartes simply says that out of rational necessity one must affirm the existence of God.

The philosophers said that the affirmation of the existence of some kind of self-existent, eternal being is necessary if you are going to be rational. You have to be irrational to deny it. Or to say it in another way, not only does the Bible declare that God is, but reason itself demands the assertion of a self-existent eternal being.

We know there is a difference between affirming the

existence of a self-existent, eternal being and affirming the God of Abraham, Isaac, and Jacob. But keep in mind that a focal point of critical assault and skepticism against biblical Christianity is against the idea of God as Creator. But in classical philosophy, the skeptics who denied Christianity or Judaism or Islam or any of the world's religions had to admit that there had to be some kind of transcendent self-existent Creator for anything to exist.

That basic foundation for all theism has been attacked vigorously in our day. If you can eliminate the idea of a necessary being, then you can eliminate creation, and if you eliminate creation, you don't have to worry about Christianity. That's what's at stake here in this debate.

Chapter Ten

Being and Transcendence

In the last chapter, we looked at certain different versions of the ontological argument for the existence of God—that is, an argument from "being." In its simplest formulation, the argument proposes that if something exists now, then something must have necessary being. That is, something must have the power to be within itself, or nothing could possibly be, but since something is, then something somewhere, somehow must have the power of being within it.

Those who have denied the existence of God have at the same time denied the idea of a necessary, eternal, self-existent being. They have argued against that idea on the basis of a doctrine of self-creation.

Some atheists did agree that it is a compelling axiom of reason that if something exists now, then something has always existed. Something must have necessary being. But they questioned, Why do you have to appeal to a transcendent God to be identified with the idea of a self-existent, necessary being? Why could it not be the universe itself?

The first answer is that there are clearly elements within the universe that manifest what we call contingency— that is, things that go through a process of generation and decay, whose existence is dependent and derived and is not independent. For example, I am a part of the universe, but these philosophers would not argue that I in my present individuated state am eternal and self-existent. It doesn't take much of an examination of R.C. Sproul to realize that he is not self-existent and does not have the power of being within himself.

Those who argue for an eternal universe of some sort will grant that some parts of the universe are not self-existent and eternal. But they usually argue that there is a pulsating core to the universe out of which everything else comes. They argue that it's only this pulsating core that has necessary being. Again, not everything in the universe is self-existent and eternal. But they say that before the big bang, there had to have been some pulsating energy or pure singularity with compression of all matter and energy into one singular point, and out of that all reality flows. And this pulsating core that does have the power of being within itself doesn't have to be located somewhere "beyond," where we speak of the transcendence of God. That is, when we speak about God, we make a distinction between God and the world, and we say that God transcends His universe. God is not the universe. God created the universe. That's the affirmation of historic Christianity. But this theory says: Why do we have to have a cause for the universe that is outside the universe? Why can't we locate it within the universe itself?

But there is a certain equivocation going on in language here. Equivocation occurs when the terms used in an argument undergo changes in their meaning. These philosophers say that there is a self-existent, eternal necessary being that causes everything, but it's not God because it's not transcendent but rather is within the universe.

The point we must grasp is that the term *transcendence* in philosophy or in theology is not a term that describes geography. When we say God is above and beyond the universe, we're not saying that there is a line up in the sky several billion or trillion miles away that defines the outer rim of the universe, and then above that line in space and time is the dwelling place of the Almighty. We're not using the term *transcendence* to speak of the "where" of God, of the residence of God. But rather, the term *transcendence*, when applied to God, means that God's being is above and beyond all created existence. Transcendence, when it is applied to God, says that God is a higher order of being, that God's being is above and beyond the type of beings that are found in the everyday world in which we live.

However, the atheistic argument that says we can have an explanation for that which exists now without an appeal to a transcendent being actually appeals to a transcendent being by differentiating this pulsating core from everything else in the universe. What is the difference between this mysterious core and everything else?

In effect, this mysterious core is the creator, and everything else is the creature. This core alone has eternal self-existence. This mysterious core has necessary being.

Everything else in the universe does not have necessary being. With respect to being, this core that gets everything going transcends everything else. These philosophers and scientists end up giving us a beautiful description of the classical description of the character of God Himself, though they are saying that God is a part of this universe.

Again, there's another subtle word game going on here. Sometimes, when we use the word *universe*, we use it to mean the whole realm of creation. At other times, the term *universe* refers to all that is. Now, if I use *universe* to describe everything that is, would the Christian affirm that God is in the universe? Yes, because if the term *universe* means everything that is, and if God is, then certainly God must be within the framework of what we're calling the universe. But if we use the term *universe* to refer to the whole created realm, would we say that God is limited to that realm? No. We would say His being cannot be contained there, that it is there, but it's beyond there as well. So again, a kind of equivocation is taking place. But our main point is that reason demands something that is self-existent and eternal, and no theory can get away from that.

Christians ought not to retreat in front of this wholesale attack that has been launched against biblical Christianity that tells us over and over again that if you're going to be scientific or if you're going to be rational or if you're going to be logical, then you have to abandon your religious faith. We don't have to retreat from those who make faith equivalent to a leap into irrationality or into the absurd. Christian philosophy has been saying for two thousand years that reason, rationality, and logic are the allies of the truth claims of Christianity, not their enemies. But in our culture, skeptics have been saying loudly to the Christian: "You only believe by faith. We don't believe because we're rational, we're logical, and we're scientific. You, on the other hand, have formed your worldview on the basis of an irrational, illogical, emotional myth."

We have been told this for so long that now we have generations of Christians saying: "Yes, that's true. But we have something that's better than reason. We have no foundation for affirming the existence of God other than our subjective desires or our mystical experiences. We have no objective grounds for asserting the truth claims of the reality of God, and we surrender all of that to a worldview that, if you examine it, is based upon sheer irrationality and sheer absurdity."

But Christians must not leave their brains in the parking

lot of the church or surrender rationality and logical coherence to an irrational system that affirms that something comes from nothing. If we want to look at mythology, let's look at the myth of self-creation. In fact, this system is so blatant in its irrationality that we wonder why intelligent people would continue to make these affirmations. Why don't people laugh when, for instance, a physicist talks about gradual spontaneous generation?

There are two basic reasons. One is that people have never thought about it. They have never asked, "How did we ever come to this place in our thinking where we're willing to assert self-creation and other such nonsense?" In other words, we have not examined the premises that have led to this nonsense. That's what Descartes did. He tried to get back to the principal beginning points of all rationality.

Another reason is that there is enormous psychological attractiveness to this. If man can affirm a universe without God, he can affirm a life that is no longer ultimately morally accountable to that God. And a person who has unresolved guilt will do everything in his power, use every trick in his imagination, and employ every weapon at his disposal intellectually to rationalize his guilt. The ultimate effort is to get rid of the Judge. If God is simply the power supply for the origin of the universe, He doesn't threaten people. We see this in the way people talk today. People will say: "I don't believe in the God of Christianity, Judaism, or Islam. I don't believe in a personal God. But I would grant that there has to be some kind of pulsating power." But that cosmic force presents no threat if it remains impersonal, because if it's impersonal, then I am not personally accountable to it. I don't have to give an account of my life, of my sins, of my virtues to the blowing of the wind or to the earthquake. But a personal, self-existent, eternal God who made me and who made me accountable to Him is the greatest threat to my soul that there is.

Chapter Eleven

Logical Inference

Logic was never invented, because logic has always been. Logic is an aspect of God Himself. And since God is eternal, and His thinking is eternally clear, coherent, and consistent, we can say that as long as God is, logic is.

In fact, one Christian philosopher made a rather strong statement concerning the prologue of John's gospel, where we read, "In the beginning was the Word, and the Word was with God, and the Word was God" (John 1:1). The Greek word that we translate as "word" is *logos*, and *logos* is the term from which the English word *logic* derives. So this Christian philosopher said that it would be a legitimate translation of John 1 to read it as "In the beginning was logic, and logic was with God, and logic was God. . . . And logic became flesh and dwelt among us" (see v. 14). Now, the Christian philosopher did not mean that the science or discipline of logic is identical with God Himself. But rather, he believed that the second person of the Trinity is the One in whom all things find their coherence and unity and consistency. He is the outward manifestation of the inward logic, as it were, of God.

The idea is that logic is related to thought, expression, and words. Words such as *biology*, *theology*, and *sociology*—having the suffix *-ology*—borrow from the Greek *logos*, or *word* or *logic*. We could say, for example, that *biology* is a word about *bios* or "life," or we could say that the study of biology is an attempt to discern the inner logic of living things, just as *psychology* seeks the inner logic of psychical things.

When we look at the discipline of logic, we recognize that it is a formal science, much like mathematics, and it functions as a kind of regulator or governor of the relationship of propositions and premises. Logic itself has no content. Pure logic reveals nothing. It gives us no information. All logic does is define the formal, rational relationship between propositions or premises. This is important, because if we think that we can learn the things of God simply from logic, we will be sadly disappointed, because logic has no content.

But if logic has no content and merely acts as a governor or describes formal relationships of propositions, what possible benefit is it to the Christian? As we said in chapter 8, logic functions as a kind of police officer on the corner walking the beat. If I am making improper inferences or deductions from the written Word of God, the officer blows his whistle and says: "Halt where you are! Halt in the name of the law!" The whistle reveals to me that I have made a mistake in my thinking.

Logic has enormous benefit for Christians, particularly when we find ourselves confused as we seek to see the coherence of sacred Scripture with itself. Let's say I interpret a passage of the Bible in such a way that it radically contrasts with or actually contradicts another part of the Bible. If we assume that the Bible is the Word of God and that God is coherent and consistent and unified and doesn't speak with a forked tongue, then as soon as I take those two passages of

Scripture and interpret them in this way, the whistle blows and tells me I have misunderstood at least one and possibly both parts of Scripture. Because if I'm understanding the things of God in a contradictory way, then I'm not really understanding them, am I? If they are contradictory, they become unintelligible. So, as a protective device to guard against making improper deductions from Scripture, logic serves a very important function.

It will be helpful to look at some elementary principles of logic so that we may see how this sort of thing works. First, let's consider the laws of immediate inference. Inferences are conclusions or deductions drawn from propositions or premises. And an *immediate* inference is that which flows necessarily, automatically without any intervening steps; it is knowledge that we gain immediately from a particular premise.

For example, in the truth tables or the laws of immediate inference, we learn that there are different kinds of propositions. One is a universal affirmative proposition. A universal affirmative is something that predicates something of every member of a given class. For example, the famous syllogism "All men are mortal" is a universal affirmative proposition. We are affirming something about every person in the class of humanity. Now if we said, "No men are kangaroos," we would be saying something negative in a universal way.

The difference between the universal and the particular is the difference between using words like *all* or *no*, which are universal terms, and *some* or any specified number less than the total, which are particular terms. If it is true that "all men are mortal," and I said, "Some men are not mortal," would that be a legitimate inference? If all men are mortal, could it be true at the same time that some men are not mortal? We would know immediately that those two statements cannot coexist. If all in the class participate in what is predicated of them, then we can't find any in that class who do not have that predicate. If all men are mortal, it could not be true that some men are not mortal. So in this case, the particular negative cannot coexist with the universal affirmative, and that's one of the rules of the laws of immediate inference.

Let's make things a bit more difficult. Suppose I said, "All men are mortal," and then I said, "Some men are mortal." Would that be a legitimate inference or an illegitimate inference? If it's true that all men are mortal, would it be true that some men are mortal? Obviously, some would be because *some* would be part of the whole. But if I was implying that some men are not mortal and came to that conclusion, then I would be violating the laws of immediate inference. But if it's true of the whole class, then it's certainly true of part of the class. So if "all men are mortal," then surely "some men are mortal" would be a legitimate conclusion.

Now if we said, "All men are mortal" and "No men are mortal," that would be false. What if we said, "Some men are mortal" and "Some men are not mortal"? Would there be a contradiction there? No. If the proposition is simply "Some men are mortal," then the corresponding proposition "Some are not" would not immediately indicate a violation.

To simplify, let's say, "Some men are bald-headed." Is it possible that there are men who are bald-headed? Yes, and if I say that *some* men are bald-headed, does it follow necessarily from that premise that *all* men are bald-headed? No. It could also be true that "some men are *not* bald-headed." It's not always as clear when you're dealing with particulars as when you're contrasting universals of negative and positive.

Another principle of logic involves the difference

between a *possible inference* and a *necessary inference*. If I say, "Some men are mortal," it is a possible inference that some men are not mortal, but is it a necessary inference? Not at all. We can apply this to the Scriptures and see how we find errors in biblical translation. John's gospel tells us that the disciples were in the upper room and that "the doors were shut . . . for fear of the Jews." But then the text says, "Jesus came and stood in their midst" (John 20:19, NKJV). Now, is it a possible inference from that text that Jesus, in His resurrected state, in His glorified body, was able to walk through doors that were shut? This is a common inference from the text. Does the text say *explicitly* that Jesus passed through the door while it was still shut? No. It's a possible inference from the text, but the text does not make it a necessary inference because there is another possibility. Perhaps the disciples were huddled together in the upper room with the doors shut for fear of the Jews, and Jesus quietly opened the door, walked in, and appeared in front of them. Now, the text doesn't say that He opened the door, just as it doesn't say that He walked through the closed door. It doesn't say anything about how Jesus got in the room. It just simply says that the door was shut and that Jesus appeared.

Some people object by questioning why the gospel writer would give the detail that the door was shut if not to communicate the idea that our Lord had the ability to pass through this solid object. But we already have the answer to that in the text itself. We're told that the door was shut for the fear of the Jews. The detail of the doors being shut is communicated to us to tell us something not about the resurrected body of Jesus but about the state of the disciples at this time.

Or perhaps John's purpose was to tell us that the door was shut because the disciples were afraid of the Jews and to make sure we got the astonishing point of Jesus' coming through that shut door while it was still shut. But we don't know, do we? John didn't tell us. So we can say that it's a possible inference that Jesus in His resurrected body had the power to pass through solid objects, but it's not a necessary inference from that text.

The Old and New Testaments contain many passages in which certain things are implied or may be reasonably inferred as possibilities. But we need to be exceedingly careful about drawing conclusions from such implications. That's why it's important to learn something about these rules of inferences and rules of logical deductions, lest we make the mistake of drawing improper conclusions from the Word of God. If the enemy can cause us to make illegitimate inferences from the Word of God, we become as putty in his hands.

Chapter Twelve

The Mind and the Scriptures

In our brief study of the Christian and the Christian mind, we have shown that Christianity is not irrational, absurd, or illogical. (Now, we can twist the Word of God and render it illogical and irrational by our careless treatment of it.) Of course, we are not saying that rationalism and Christianity are the same thing. But Christianity is rational, and the Word of God has been given to us so that we may understand it. The word *understand* is a key term. We remember the Apostolic injunction "In malice be babes, but in *understanding* be mature" (1 Cor. 14:20, NKJV).

I often hear that people want to have a childlike faith, and they use that as a shield to protect themselves from the arduous task of applying their mind to the most accurate possible understanding of what God has given to us in His Word. But to be mature and adult in our understanding not only requires that we have an awareness and knowledge of the content of Scripture, but it also means that we need to have a coherent understanding of what we learn from Scripture; that which is incoherent is unintelligible, and that which is unintelligible is simply not understood.

In the last chapter we looked at Jesus' appearance in the upper room. Another text to consider is 1 John 5:16: "If anyone sees his brother committing a sin not leading to death, he shall ask, and God will give him life—to those who commit sins that do not lead to death. There is sin that leads to death; I do not say that one should pray for that." A basic message in this verse is that if you see your brother sinning, and the sin is not a sin unto death, you're supposed to pray for him. There is a clear admonition to pray for the brothers and sisters of the faith who have fallen into a certain sin.

But then John complicates this instruction by saying that there is a sin that leads to death. He doesn't define what that sin unto death is (and we're going to leave that mystery to the side), but presumably the people who received this epistle knew what that sin was. Is John telling them that if you see your brother or sister committing that sin, don't pray for them? No. John does not say you are not allowed to pray for somebody who is sinning the sin that leads to death. What he does say is this: "If you see your brother or sister sinning a sin that is not unto death, you *must* pray for them. But if you see them sinning a sin that is unto death, I will not say that you must pray for them."

If John says, "I am not going to say that you *must*," does that mean, therefore, you must *not*? In other words, if I say you don't have to do something, is that equivalent to saying you are *not allowed* to do it? No, we understand that something may be optional. You *may* do it, or you may *not* do it. There is a difference between saying "must" and "must not." One is a positive command; the other one is a clear prohibition. But in this case, we get a positive command to pray for those who don't sin the sin that leads to death, but what is absent in this text is a parallel absolute prohibition against praying for those who do commit this particular sin. John simply said, "I'm not going to tell you that you *must*." The text leaves it to our judgment.

Another text to consider is John 3:16. When discussing God's sovereign election with others, people usually counter with, "But doesn't the Bible say that God so loved the world that He gave His only Son, that whoever believes in Him should not perish but have eternal life?" I say: "Yes. *Whoever* believes.'" Whoever does that will not perish, and he or she will have eternal life. If we translated that into logical propositions, then we would say that all who believe (which is a universal affirmation) will have eternal life. And, to put it in the negative, none who has eternal life will perish. The perishing and the eternal life are polar opposites here in terms of the consequences of belief. Whoever does *A* (believes) will not have *B* (perish) but will have *C* (eternal life).

We also ought to consider what this text says about having the ability within ourselves to believe in Jesus Christ. What does it say? Absolutely nothing. All the text says is that "whoever does *A* will have *C* and not have *B*." It doesn't tell us anything about who will believe. Jesus later said in the gospel of John, "No one can come to me unless the Father who sent me draws him" (John 6:44). Here we have a universal negative that describes ability. No person has the ability to come to Jesus unless some condition is met by God. Some say that John 3:16 states that anybody can come to Jesus with or without any action by God. I like to point out that John 3:16 is in the same chapter where Jesus said that unless a person is born again, born of water and the Spirit, he can't enter the kingdom of God.

As we near the end of our study of the Christian mind, we want to look at an important doctrine called the noetic effects of sin. *Noetic* derives from the Greek word *nous*, which means "mind." So the noetic effect of sin is the effect that the fall or sin has on our minds. In Romans 1, Paul tells us how our foolish minds can become darkened. Historical theology concludes that the whole human person, in all faculties, has been ravaged by the corruption of human nature. Our bodies die because of sin. The impact of sin on our eyes means that as we age, our eyes grow dim. We will lose our capacity for hearing. We also know that the human will is in a state of moral bondage, captive to the evil desires and impulses of the soul.

Not only that, but the sinful heart is such that man by nature will not have God in his thinking. We have a reprobate mind, a mindset by which we are prejudiced against the sweetness of God. We know how prejudice can distort thinking. We find it difficult to understand clear ideas when we are blinded by our prejudice. Even our very ability to think at all has been severely weakened by the fall.

However, though we are fallen, we still have the ability to think and make choices. We still have the faculty of choosing. We still have a will. We can still think. Of course, we are all prone to error. But a person does not have to be a Christian to be a great mathematician. Nor does a person have to be a Christian to be a master logician. This is because the skill of reasoning in a logical fashion is not something that is simply inherent, where you have it or you don't have it. The skill of reasoning in an orderly, logical, sound, and cogent fashion can be learned and developed.

As Christians, we want to think with the utmost cogency and clarity. As a matter of discipline, it would be much to our benefit to study and master the elementary principles of reasoning so that we can, to a certain degree, overcome the ravages of sin on our thinking. As long as sin is in us, we will never become perfect in our reasoning. Sin prejudices us against the law of God, and we have to fight to overcome these basic distortions of the truth of God. But if we love God not only with all our hearts but with all our minds and we yield our minds to Him and devote our minds to Him, we will be rigorous in our attempts to be as accurate as humanly possible when we come to His Word.

The Scriptures exhort us to search them, to read them carefully. We are to drink deeply at the fountain of the living Word of God. Christian, you are called to think as a Christian. We are to pursue the very mind of Christ. Part of the perfect humanity of our Lord Himself is that Jesus of Nazareth never made an illegitimate inference. He never jumped to a conclusion that was unwarranted by the premises. His thinking was crystal clear. His thinking was coherent. His thinking was sound. Never has the world experienced such sound thinking as that which was manifest in the mind of Christ.

As we are called to imitate our Lord, I plead with you to make it a matter of chief and earnest business in your life to love Him with all your mind.

About the Author

Dr. R.C. Sproul was founder of Ligonier Ministries, founding pastor of Saint Andrew's Chapel in Sanford, Fla., first president of Reformation Bible College, and executive editor of *Tabletalk* magazine. His radio program, *Renewing Your Mind*, is still broadcast daily on hundreds of radio stations around the world and can also be heard online. He was author of more than one hundred books, including *The Holiness of God*, *Chosen by God*, and *Everyone's a Theologian*. He was recognized throughout the world for his articulate defense of the inerrancy of Scripture and the need for God's people to stand with conviction upon His Word.

Free eBooks *by* R.C. Sproul

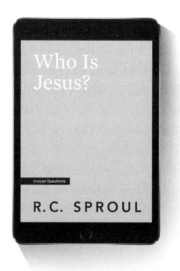

Does prayer really change things? Can I be sure I'm saved? Dr. R.C. Sproul answers these important questions, along with more than thirty others, in his Crucial Questions series. Designed for the Christian or thoughtful inquirer, these booklets can be used for personal study, small groups, and conversations with family and friends. Browse the collection and download your free digital ebooks today.

Get 3 free months of *Tabletalk*

In 1977, R.C. Sproul started *Tabletalk* magazine.

Today it has become the most widely read subscriber-based monthly

devotional magazine in the world. **Try it free for 3 months.**

ASK LIGONIER

Do we have free will?

Is it true that God controls everything?

Does prayer change things?

A Place to Find Answers

Maybe you're leading a Bible study tomorrow. Maybe you're just beginning to dig deeper. It's good to know that you can always ask Ligonier. For more than fifty years, Christians have been looking to Ligonier Ministries, the teaching fellowship of R.C. Sproul, for clear and helpful answers to biblical and theological questions. Now you can ask those questions online as they arise, confident that our team will work quickly to provide clear, concise, and trustworthy answers. The *Ask Ligonier* podcast provides another avenue for you to submit questions to some of the most trusted pastors and teachers who are serving the church today. When you have questions, just ask Ligonier.

FOR MORE INFORMATION, VISIT ASK.LIGONIER.ORG